HAPPY EVER CRAFTER

ANIMALS

ANNALEES LIM

WAYLAND
www.waylandbooks.co.uk

First published in Great Britain in 2018 by Wayland
Copyright © Hodder and Stoughton 2018

Senior Commissioning Editor: Melanie Palmer
Design: Square and Circus
Illustrations: Supriya Sahai

Additional illustrations: Freepik

HB ISBN 978 1 5263 0759 0
PB ISBN 978 1 5263 0760 6

MIX
Paper from
responsible sources
FSC® C104740
FSC
www.fsc.org

Printed in China

Wayland
An imprint of
Hachette Children's Group
Part of Hodder and Stoughton
Carmelite House
50 Victoria Embankment
London EC4Y 0DZ

An Hachette UK Company
www.hachette.co.uk

SAFETY INFORMATION:
Please ask an adult for help with any activities
that could be tricky, involve cooking or handling
glass. Ask adult permission when appropriate.

Due care has been taken to ensure the activities
are safe and the publishers regret they cannot
accept liability for any loss or injuries sustained.

CONTENTS

Animal Kingdom

The animal kingdom is vast – you will find animals in every country and ocean on the planet. They can be divided into different types such as mammals, birds, fish, reptiles and insects and then divided again into vertebrates and invertebrates.

A vertebrate means any animal that has a backbone. There are thousands of different species of vertebrates including some fish, birds and mammals.

Invertebrate describes animals that don't have a backbone but may have skeleton-like armour on the outside of their body. This includes insects, snails and lots of things that live under the sea. There are over a million different species of invertebrates and there are still more being discovered.

FACT!

The most famous extinct animal is the dodo. Although it died out many years ago, around the 17th century, it still remains a symbol of what happens when we don't look after the planet's animals.

Zoologists study animals to find out about how they live, what they eat and which types of environments they thrive in. This book is perfect for any animal lover. You will find out lots of fun facts about many different kinds of animals and you'll get to make some great crafts, too. There are even fun ideas about how to plan a really wild party that will end up being a roaring success!

TOP TIP

There is a list of over 700 endangered animals who are close to being extinct, such as sea turtles, tigers, elephants and gorillas. You can do your bit to help save these animals in lots of different ways. You can support charities and local conservation projects or just try to make these craft activities as environmentally friendly as possible. Did you know that tonnes of plastic bags and bottles end up in the sea every year? Creatures who live in the sea often get trapped in the waste or even try and eat it, which is very damaging to their health. By recycling any plastic and turning it into wonderful crafts, you will be helping the environment, too.

CUTE CREATURE COSTUMES

These four fancy dress projects are perfect if you have a party to go to, if you're starring in an animal-themed show or if you just love dressing up! Collect materials from around your house – upcycle and reuse them, and turn them into fantastically wild costumes.

RHINOCEROS

There are five species of rhino that live in the wild in Asia and Africa. These large, heavy animals love to eat plants. They have thick skin that is really sensitive so they cover it in mud to help stop insect bites and sunburn.

YOU WILL NEED:

- GREY PAINT (ACRYLIC OR THICK POSTER PAINT IS IDEAL) • PAINTBRUSH
- OLD BASEBALL CAP • LIGHT AND DARK GREY FABRIC • WHITE PAPER
- SCISSORS • FABRIC GLUE
- PERMANENT MARKER PEN

1. Paint an old baseball cap grey using paint that has not been watered down. Leave it to dry.

2. Cut out two small ear shapes from some light grey fabric, and two larger ear shapes from some darker grey fabric. You can paint any scrap fabric you have if you do not have the right colour.

3. Cut out a small half circle shape from some white paper and roll into a cone.

4. Stick the ears and cone on to the hat with the fabric glue.

5. Use a permanent marker pen to draw on eyes and a mouth.

COMPLETE THE COSTUME!

Wear all grey and attach a small fabric tail to the back of your top with a safety pin so that you can remove it easily.

ELEPHANT

The African and Asian elephant might look similar, but you can tell the difference by their ears. The African elephant has large, wide ears that are a similar shape to the continent the animals come from, whereas the Asian elephant has smaller ears that are more rounded at the top. Which species will you choose to make?

YOU WILL NEED:

- TWO LARGE CEREAL BOXES • SCISSORS
- GREY PAINT • PAINTBRUSH • WHITE CRAFT GLUE • WHITE PAPER • BLACK PEN

1. Cut the top off the cereal box and cut a 'U' shape out of the front.

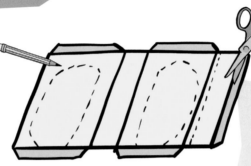

2. Cut two ears out from the front and back of another cereal box.

3. Use the side of the cereal box to make the trunk.

FACT
Elephants can suck up to 14 litres of water into their trunk. They will use it to drink or blow on to themselves to wash or cool down.

4. Stick the ears and trunk to the first cereal box and paint it all grey.

5. Stick on two eyes and tusks made from white paper to the top of the box.

Where does an elephant pack its clothes when it goes on holiday?

It's trunk!

OCTOPUS

There are about 300 different species of octopus. Did you know that they all have beaks and three hearts? The name has the word 'octo' (which means eight) because of the number of arms each octopus has. People often mistakenly call the arms tentacles.

YOU WILL NEED:

• OLD T-SHIRT AND TROUSERS • 4 PAIRS OF LONG SOCKS • SCISSORS • NEWSPAPER • PERMANENT MARKER PENS • PAPER • WHITE CRAFT GLUE

1. Draw a head and eyes on to the t-shirt using the marker pens.

2. Cut off the waist band from some old trousers (you can use the rest of the material for other craft projects).

3. Stuff the old long socks with scrunched up pieces of newspaper, leaving 10 cm at the top. You will need eight in total.

4. Glue some small paper circles to the bottom of the arms to make the suckers.

FACT!
The word 'animal' comes from the Latin word 'animalis' which means 'living being'.

5. Cut a slit at the top of the arms and use the two sections to tie each one on to the waist band. Space all eight evenly around the band.

BLUE WHALE

Blue whales are the largest living animals on the planet and can grow up to 100 feet – that's as long as two buses put together, and they have hearts the size of a small car! Their mouths are so large that they can hold 90 tonnes of food and water but their preferred food is krill. Krill is a small, prawn-like animal that is only a few centimetres long, so blue whales will eat about 40 million of them a day!

YOU WILL NEED:
- LARGE CARDBOARD BOX • SCISSORS
- BLUE PAINT • PAINTBRUSH • FABRIC
- STAPLER • STICKY TAPE • COLOURED MARKER PENS

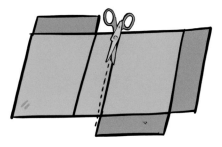

1. Flatten out a cardboard box and cut in half.

2. Draw and cut out two whale body shapes and paint blue. Once dry, tape the two whale shapes together at each end.

3. Draw on details such as the eyes, blow hole and throat pleats.

4. Bend the card so that it is shaped like a body. Staple two lengths of fabric to each shape. Make sure they are long enough to fit over your shoulders.

PARTY ANIMAL

Planning a great party doesn't have to be a chore and it won't take you long to get organised if you follow these simple tips. If you can't take a trip to the zoo, then make the zoo come to you. With these craft projects, recipes and games everyone will be sure to have a really wild time!

PERFECT PLANNING

It may seem like there are a million things to do to get ready for your party, but if you break it down by writing a list of all the important things, you'll soon be ready for the big day. Keep a list of what needs to be done so nothing gets forgotten. You'll need to think about these things:

HABITATS: A habitat is the home of an animal. You can also create the perfect environment for your friends. Use the projects on page 16 to transform your party space into a familly—friendly zoo.

MAMMAL MAKES: There are so many different species in the animal kingdom that you could spend years making them all. Turn to page 28 to find four projects to start you off. Make them as extra decorations for your zoo, or give them out as prizes to the winners of the games you play.

FEEDING TIME: Make sure you have plenty of snacks ready to feed your hungry horde! Follow the recipes on page 20 to make tasty treats, all with an animal theme.

MONKEYING AROUND: Parties are not complete without playing a few games. There are lots of fun ideas on page 12 for you to play, and they are fun to make, too.

ZOO CREW!

Use this template to make this zoo-style invitation. Remember to include all the key information so that your guests have all they need to know to get to your party.

To:
Write the name of your zookeeper friend here.

What:
Say who is celebrating and why!

YOU ARE INVITED...

To: _____

What: _____

When: _____
_____

Dress code: _____   RSVP: _____

When and Where:
Date, Time and Address of the party.

Dress code:
Say if you want people to turn up in fancy dress.

RSVP:
Ask people to let you know if they can come.

PARTY GAMES

If you don't want your guests to run wild at your party, then these games will help keep everyone entertained. Each game is simple to play and easy to make so you can get your guests to help, too.

CHEATING CHEETAHS

A cheetah is a spotted animal and is part of the cat family. It is the fastest animal that lives on land, making it one of the world's deadliest predators. A cheetah uses its long tail as a rudder when it runs, helping it steer and keep its balance.

YOU WILL NEED:

- 2 CEREAL BOXES • WRAPPING PAPER • PLAIN PAPER • SCISSORS • GLUE STICK • COLOURED PENS

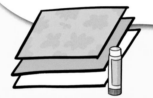

1. Cover one side of the card with old wrapping paper and the other with white/plain paper. Repeat 3 more times.

2. Cut up each sheet into 10 small cards. You will need 40 cards to play the game.

3. Draw a zebra pattern on 5 cards.

4. Make 7 more sets of 5 cards – cheetah spots, peacock feathers, giraffe markings, fish scales, panda patterns, tiger stripes and crocodile skin.

HOW TO PLAY

Each player starts with 4 cards and the rest are stacked in the middle. When it is your turn you can choose to lay 2, 3 or 4 cards down. They must be matching for you to put them down, or you can choose to lie about it. Tell the group what they are but keep them face down so no one can see them. If people think you're lying they can shout, 'Cheating Cheetah'. If you were lying, you have to pick up all the cards that were put down. If you were telling the truth, then the person who shouted out picks them up. If you don't want to, or don't have enough cards to put down, pick up one card from the stack. The first player to put down all their cards wins.

CHEEKY MONKEYS

Most monkeys, like humans, eat both plants and animals. They like to live on the ground and up high in tall trees. They are often confused with apes but you can tell it's a monkey by checking if it's got a tail. Tails help them to balance and grip on to the trees.

YOU WILL NEED:
• PAPER PLATES • YELLOW PAINT
• BROWN MARKER PEN • SCISSORS
• PAINTBRUSH

1. Paint 5 plates yellow and leave to dry.

2. Cut out banana shapes from the edge of the plates. You should get three from each plate.

3. Use the brown pen to add markings and a stalk.

HOW TO PLAY

This is a race to see who can collect the most bananas in the fastest time. Peg the bananas on to a washing line. Make a starting line that everyone stands behind. Work in pairs to collect the most bananas. When the timer starts, link arms with your partner and race to the washing line. You can only use one hand each. One person takes off the peg, and the other takes the banana. Collect the bananas in a pile at the starting line. The timer stops when there are no more bananas to collect.

FLAMINGO BALANCE

Flamingoes are tall, brightly-coloured birds with long legs. They are born with grey or white feathers which slowly change colour over time depending on what they have been eating, and can range from pink to red or orange. They can fly as well as swim, but are often seen wading or standing on one leg in shallow waters.

YOU WILL NEED:
- WHITE PAPER • SCISSORS
- BLACK FELT-TIP PEN • HOLE PUNCH
- STRING/RIBBON/ELASTIC

1. Fold a piece of paper in half.

2. Draw a beak shape and cut it out.

3. Colour the end of the beak black with a felt-tip pen.

4. Punch some holes in the corners of the beak.

5. Thread some ribbon, string or elastic through the holes.

HOW TO PLAY
Everyone who wants to play wears a beak. Everyone stands on one leg at the same time and tries not to wobble. The last person still standing on one leg is the winner.

PANDA POTS

Giant pandas are well known for their black and white fur and love for eating bamboo. Did you know that, unlike the rest of the bear family, they never hibernate? When the winter comes they just climb down to where it is warmer and continue to eat the bamboo that they love.

What is a cheetah's favourite thing to eat?
Fast Food

YOU WILL NEED:
- COLOURED PAPER • FELT-TIP PENS
- WHITE PLASTIC CUPS • PAPER
- SCISSORS • GLUE STICK

1. Draw a panda shape on to some paper and cut it out.

2. Glue it around a pot. Repeat so that you have made 5 pots.

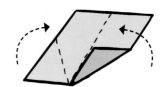

3. Fold pieces of paper like paper planes to make small darts.

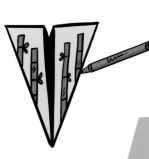

4. Draw a bamboo pattern on to the paper darts.

HOW TO PLAY
Spread the pots around on the ground or a table. Take turns to throw your coloured bamboo darts into the pots. Whoever gets the most darts into the pots is the winner. Make it more difficult by moving the pots further away or making them different heights.

IN THE ZOO

Welcome your guests into a zoo that you've built full of wild animals. These projects are a great start and you can add more to make your zoo bigger. Each animal needs a different space to live in. You could create dry deserts for the snakes and green jungles for the gorillas.

FEEDING TIME

Animals that live in zoos can't hunt for food in the same way they would in the wild. It's a zookeeper's job to know what each animal likes to eat and when. Fruit bats like fruit and seals love fish, whereas tigers eat meat that needs to be hidden first so they don't get lazy.

YOU WILL NEED:
- PLASTIC BOTTLE • TIN FOIL
- STICKY TAPE • PAPER • SCISSORS

1. Cut a clean plastic bottle in half and wrap in tin foil.

2. Wrap a strip of paper in more tin foil and wrap around the edge of the bottle.

3. Make a handle from some more coloured paper and stick on.

4. Cut out letters to spell 'feed' and stick them on the front of the bucket.

HOW TO PLAY
Use these buckets as serving dishes. Put sweet or savoury snacks in them and display them together on your snack table.

BIRDS OF PARADISE

This group of exotic birds are usually found in the rainforests of Indonesia, Papua New Guinea and Australia. Unlike most birds they make nests on the ground. The males have very colourful feathers that they use to attract females and some even do a dance, too.

YOU WILL NEED:
- FIZZY DRINK CANS • COLOURED PAPER OR MAGAZINES • STICKY TAPE
- SCISSORS • OPTIONAL: STRING
- GOOGLY EYES

1. Cover the lid and wrap the fizzy drink can in paper.

2. Stick a yellow paper rim on to the top of the can and cut a 'V' shape into each side to make the beak.

3. Cut lots of feathers out from the different coloured paper. Brightly-coloured pictures in magazines are the best to use.

4. Make two paper feet from yellow paper.

5. Stick on the feathers and feet to the can. Add googly eyes.

TOP TIP
Tie some string round the middle of the cans so that the birds can be hung up to look like they are flying.

POINT THE WAY

Signposts are useful in zoos – they help you get to where you want to go. This craft will help you point your guests towards the food, tell them where the games are or to just welcome people to your party.

YOU WILL NEED:

- THICK CARD • BROWN PAINT
- PAINTBRUSH • PEN OR PENCIL
- BLACK MARKER PEN • STRING

TOP TIP

Hang lots of signs together, pointing in different directions. Use a coat stand, door handles or hang them from hooks.

1. Cut an arrow shape from some thick card.

2. Paint some wood grain on the card with some brown paint.

3. Use a pencil or pen to make two holes at the top of the arrow.

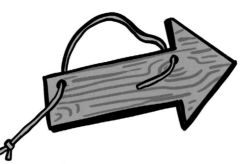

4. Thread some string through the holes and tie in place.

FACT!

Did you know that horses and cows sleep standing up?

5. Write your words on to the arrow using the black permanent marker pen.

MAPS

Every zoo has a map to show where all the different animal enclosures are. Use this project to plan where your party zones will be or use it as a wall decoration. During the party, people can draw their favourite animals on paper and stick them to the map. This is a great souvenir of the day for you to keep.

YOU WILL NEED:
- LARGE SHEET OF PAPER • PAINT
- PAINTBRUSH • PAPER • PENS
- SCISSORS • STICKY TAPE • GLUE STICK

1. Cut out a large piece of paper. Flatten out cardboard boxes, packaging or join smaller pieces of paper together with sticky tape.

2. Paint the whole piece of paper in different shades of green and leave to dry.

3. Use yellow paint to draw wiggly lines all over the paper that will be the paths around your zoo.

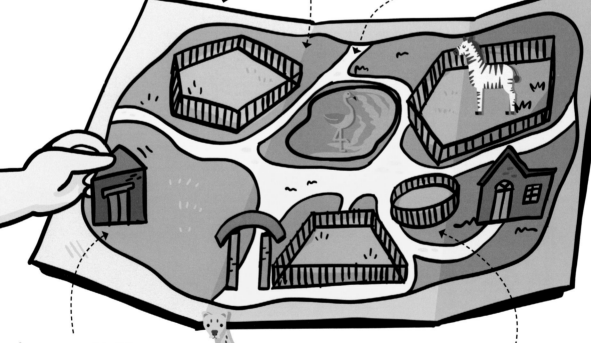

4. Draw small buildings on pieces of paper. Cut them out and stick around the map. These could be gift shops or ticket offices.

5. Use pens to create enclosures, ready for your animals to live in.

TASTY TREATS

No one will be left hungry with these four delicious recipes that will fit in perfectly with your animal themed party. Remember to wash your hands before you start and ask an adult to help you.

DOG BOWL BISCUITS

Dogs are a very popular domestic pet even though they are descended from wolves. They have a great sense of smell that is about 1,000 times better than ours, which is why you will find them often sniffing things out, especially delicious treats.

YOU WILL NEED:

- PAPER BOWL • CARD • SCISSORS
- STICKY TAPE • PENCIL • PAINT
- PAINTBRUSH

1. Cut the bottom out of a paper bowl.

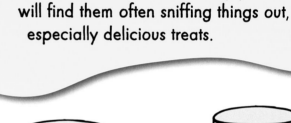

2. Make a card circle so that it fits in the hole you've just cut out.

3. Draw around this on to some more card, to make the base.

3. Stick the parts together to make the dog bowl.

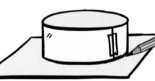

4. Paint in a bright colour, leaving a bone shape on the front.

5. Use icing pens to draw bone shapes on to your favourite biscuits. Leave the icing to set before serving them in the dog bowl.

TROPICAL FISH PUNCH

Tropical water is warm and can be found around the equator. Here you will find tropical fish living in large groups called schools – there are thousands of different species, most are very brightly coloured with different patterns. People like to keep tropical fish as pets as they are pretty to look at. They have to live in special tanks with heaters so they don't get cold.

YOU WILL NEED:

- CLEAR PLASTIC CUPS • SAND
- WHITE CRAFT GLUE • GREEN PAPER OR PLASTIC BAGS • PERMANENT MARKER PENS • STRAWS • SCISSORS
- STICKY TAPE

1. Paint some white craft glue on to the bottom of the plastic cups and dip in sand.

2. Use permanent marker pens to decorate the cups with tropical fish.

3. Cut out leaf shapes from green paper or plastic bags.

4. Fix on to the top of straws with sticky tape.

FRUIT PUNCH RECIPE

You can mix your favourite fruits and juices together to make any punch you like or mix together the following for an ocean-like drink: Carefully crush blackberries in a bowl. Pour in some lemonade, elderflower cordial and ice cubes and stir well before serving in the cups.

CACTUS CAKES

The desert is a very dry, hot and sandy environment that often gets very cold at night. This means only certain plants and animals live there, and they all have their own special ways to keep cool and find water to survive.

YOU WILL NEED:
- PRE-MADE CUPCAKES • GREEN WATER ICING • LADY FINGER BISCUITS • GREASEPROOF PAPER • ICING PENS • BUTTER ICING • BISCUITS • JELLY SNAKES

1. Mix together some green icing and dip in the lady finger biscuit. Leave to set.

2. Use the icing pen to add details to the cactus.

3. Mix together some butter icing and cover the top of the cupcake.

4. Press the cactus into the cupcake.

5. Sprinkle some crushed biscuits over the butter icing and decorate with some jelly snakes.

PENGUIN POPS

YOU WILL NEED:
- PLASTIC CUPS (OR ICE LOLLY MOULDS)
- CLING FILM • MILK CHOCOLATE
- PUFFED WHEAT CEREAL
- LOLLY STICKS/WOODEN SKEWERS
- ICING PENS

It's a common mistake to think that penguins live in the North Pole and only like the freezing cold. Most penguins live in the southern half of the world, in countries such as South Africa, Australia and Peru. They are keen swimmers and dive to great depths, using their wings as flippers to help them move through the water to catch fish.

1. Line the plastic cups with some cling film.

2. Melt some milk chocolate into a bowl and mix in some cereal.

3. Spoon the mixture into the cups and press in the lolly stick. Leave to set.

4. Remove the cups and peel off the cling film.

TO SERVE

Empty a bag of flour into a bowl and press it down firmly with the back of a spoon. Press the Penguin Pops into the flour so that it looks like they are gliding across the ice.

5. Decorate with icing pens to make the penguin. You will need eyes, a beak, wings and feet.

CREATURE CRAFTS

Animal spotting is easy to do and inspires fantastic crafts. Look around pet shops, go for a walk in the countryside, watch birds in a park or garden or even visit the zoo. Try out these projects and discover ways to adapt them yourself and make your favourite creatures from the animal kingdom.

UNDER THE SEA

YOU WILL NEED:
• CARD • SCISSORS • PLASTIC BAGS
• GLUE STICK • DARK COLOURED PAPER

Oceans are huge and the deeper you go, the darker and colder it gets. There are lots of creatures that have learned to survive in deep water by collecting food that falls from above, or by lighting up their bodies to help them see in the dark. It's a hard place for humans to explore but more creatures are being discovered each time we dive.

1. Make two rectangular frames from thin card.

2. Cut out wavy strips from plastic bags.

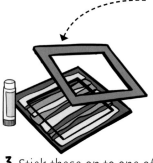

4. Glue the other frame on top, sandwiching the plastic layers in between

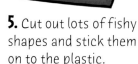

5. Cut out lots of fishy shapes and stick them on to the plastic.

3. Stick these on to one of the frames, making sure they overlap slightly.

TOP TIP
Stick this on to the window so that the light shines through it and you can see the fish silhouettes swimming in the sunlight.

CAT CUSHION

Cats make great pets and are very playful creatures, although you will mostly find them napping. Did you know they can sleep for about 16-18 hours a day? This cushion craft is a purr-fect present for any cat lover and great to cuddle up with when you're falling asleep.

YOU WILL NEED:

- AN OLD JUMPER • SCISSORS
- NEEDLE AND THREAD
- STUFFING AND CUSHION PAD

1. Sew up the neck and cuff of one sleeve.

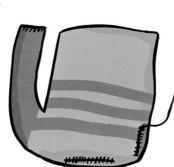

2. Tuck the other sleeve inside the body and sew up the hole.

3. First fill the sleeve with stuffing, then the body with a cushion pad. Sew up the bottom of the jumper.

4. Cut out a nose, eyes, whiskers, ears and paws from scrap fabric or felt.

MEOW!

5. Stick or sew these on to the cushion.

Why are fish so smart? Because they love to hang out in schools.

FARMYARD

YOU WILL NEED:
- LARGE PIECE OF CARD • GREEN PAINT
- PAINTBRUSH • PAPER • SCISSORS
- STICKY TAPE • SMALL CARDBOARD
BOX • RED AND WHITE PAINT • DARK
COLOURED CARD • GLUE STICK

Farmers grow plants and look after animals. They have lots of land that is surrounded by fences to stop the animals from escaping. Grow your farm by making different paddocks that will sit next to this one, and fill them with your favourite farmyard animals.

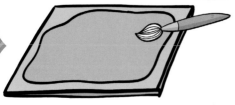

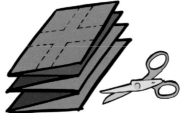

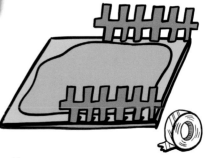

1. Paint a large sheet of cardboard green and leave to dry.

2. Fold a long strip of brown paper into six equal parts and draw a cross on the front, making sure it touches the sides.

3. Cut out the cross shape and open it up. Stick it around the edge of the green cardboard. Make enough to go round the whole edge.

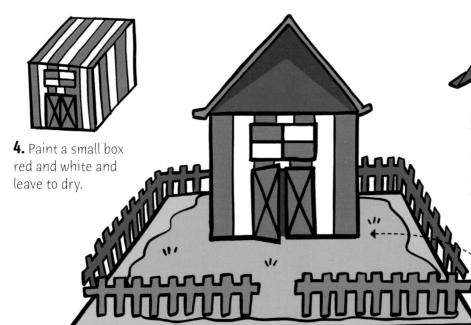

4. Paint a small box red and white and leave to dry.

5. Fold a piece of dark card in half and stick on to make the roof, and cut some slits in to make the door open.

6. Stick the barn in the field.

WISE OWL POTS

Owls come out at night and they have large eyes to help them see. Unlike most birds, they do not make their own nests. Instead, they prefer to hide in holes in trees or even use old nests that other birds have made.

YOU WILL NEED:
- LARGE PLASTIC BOTTLE • SCISSORS
- STICKY TAPE • WHITE CRAFT GLUE
- COLOURED PAPER • PEN

1. Draw a line around the middle of the plastic bottle with two triangles on top.

2. Cut this out carefully and cover the edges with sticky tape so they are not sharp.

3. Cover with a layer of white craft glue and stick on torn bits of paper. Leave to dry.

4. Cut out some paper shapes for the eyes, wings and beak.

IT'S A HOOT!

5. Glue the shapes on to the bottle base and cover the whole thing with another layer of white craft glue.

SHARK SOFTIE

There are hundreds of species of shark. Most of them are not scary at all, despite some having up to 3,000 teeth. There are no vegetarian sharks but this does not mean that we are on the menu. Shark attacks on humans are rare and most have no interest in hurting us.

YOU WILL NEED:
• FABRIC • SCISSORS • PAPER
• PENCIL • FABRIC GLUE

1. Draw a shark shape on a piece of paper and cut it out.

2. Use the paper shark as a template and cut out two shapes from some fabric.

3. Put fabric glue around most of the edge of one piece of fabric and place the other piece of fabric on top. Leave to dry.

Why does a cow eat grass all day long?

Because it thinks it is a Lawn Moo-er

4. Stuff the shark with scrap fabric and glue together the gap.

5. Decorate with more scrap fabric to make fins, eyes and teeth.

PORCUPINE PRINT

Porcupines are nocturnal animals which means they like to be awake at night. They eat mainly plants but some larger animals prey on them. To protect themselves they use the thousands of sharp sticks on their backs, called quills, as armour.

YOU WILL NEED:
- BROWN AND WHITE PAINT • GLUE STICK • PAINTBRUSH • THICK PAPER • PAINT PALLET • SMALL TWIG • BLACK PEN • GOOGLY EYE

1. Paint a brown porcupine body on to a piece of thick paper.

2. Spread out white and brown paint on to a flat surface such as a paint pallet.

3. Dip the twig into the paint and print it on to the back of the body. Leave to dry.

4. Use a black pen to draw details such as the nose, mouth, arms and legs.

5. Stick on a googly eye to finish.

MEERKAT FINGER PAINTING

Meerkats are small mammals from Africa that live in very large groups called clans or mobs. They are very protective of the place they live and leave a scent to mark their territory which includes lots of underground tunnels. You might see them stand on their back legs when looking out for predators while the others are busy looking for food.

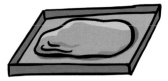

1. Mix up some light brown paint and spread it evenly on a pallet.

2. Press your finger into the paint and make a print on to a sheet of paper.

YOU WILL NEED:
- LIGHT BROWN PAINT • PAINT PALLET
- PAINTBRUSH • PAPER • SCISSORS
- GLUE STICK • FELT-TIP PENS

3. Use your thumb to make another print on top of the first. Leave to dry.

4. Cut out a tail, arms, feet, a nose and ears from paper.

5. Glue the paper parts on to the fingerprints and draw on any smaller details like the eyes and markings.

SWIMMING SEA TURTLE

Most sea turtles have hard shells that protect their bodies. They swim long distances through the ocean and often face many dangers, one of which is pollution from plastic. They mistake this for food and eat it by mistake.

YOU WILL NEED:
• A PLASTIC BOTTLE • SCISSORS
• STICKY TAPE • DARK AND LIGHT GREEN PAPER • LIGHT GREEN AND BLUE TISSUE PAPER • WHITE CRAFT GLUE • PAINTBRUSH

1. Cut off the bottom of the plastic bottle and cover the edges with a strip of sticky tape.

2. Make a head and 4 fins from dark green paper and stick them on to the smaller plastic bottle.

3. Tear up small pieces of lighter green tissue paper and stick them on to the bottle. Repeat with blue tissue on to the larger bottle. Leave to dry.

TOP TIP
This craft is great for reducing the amount of plastic waste you throw away!

4. Cover the base of the larger bottle with long green seaweed, curling some down.

5. Balance the turtle on top of the larger bottle to make it look like it is swimming through the seaweed.

ANIMAL PUZZLE
CAN YOU FIND THE ANSWERS TO THESE QUESTIONS?

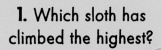

1. Which sloth has climbed the highest?

2. How many flowers can you count?

3. Where is the parrot hiding?

4. Which sloth is the odd one out?

ANSWERS: 1. C **2.** 10 **3.** Behind the middle tree. **4.** D – the sleeping sloth

DISCOVER MORE...

HAPPY EVER CRAFTER KNIGHTS AND CASTLES

JAMMED FULL OF CRAFT ACTIVITIES!

978 1 5263 0753 8

Realm of Knights and Castles
Kingdom of Costumes
King of the Castle
Invitations
Party Games
Party Decorations
Fantastic Feasts
Medieval Makes
Knights Puzzle

HAPPY EVER CRAFTER ROBOTS AND ALIENS

JAMMED FULL OF CRAFT ACTIVITIES!

978 1 5263 0755 2

Sci-Fi Worlds
Outer Space Outfits
Planet Party
Intergalactic Invites
Party Games
Party Decorations
Space Food
Crafty Makes
Space Puzzle

HAPPY EVER CRAFTER FAIRY TALES

JAMMED FULL OF CRAFT ACTIVITIES!

978 1 5263 0751 4

Once Upon a Time
Costumes and Characters
Enchanted Accessories
Invitations
Party Games
Party Food
Party Decorations
Crafty Makes
Fairy Puzzle

HAPPY EVER CRAFTER PIRATES

JAMMED FULL OF CRAFT ACTIVITIES!

978 1 5263 0713 2

Argh M' Hearties!
Daring Dressing Up
Pirate Plans
Invitations
Party Games
Party Decorations
Party Food
Crafty Makes
Pirate Puzzle

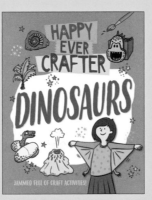

HAPPY EVER CRAFTER DINOSAURS

JAMMED FULL OF CRAFT ACTIVITIES!

978 1 5263 0757 6

Dinosaur World
Big Beasts Fancy Dress
Prehistoric Party Plans
Invitations
Party Games
Party Decorations
Party Food
Craft-o-saurus
Dinosaur Puzzle

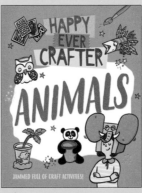

HAPPY EVER CRAFTER ANIMALS

JAMMED FULL OF CRAFT ACTIVITIES!

978 1 5263 0759 0

Amazing Animals
Cute Creature Costumes
Party Animal
Invitations
Party Games
In the Zoo
Tasty Treats
Creature Crafts
Animals Puzzle

WAYLAND
www.waylandbooks.co.uk